b
_____
_____
_____

Check
capital letter H   gaps
full stop .   pp ed

Activity 6
Build a sentence

ruin _____
_____
_____
_____
_____

Activity 7
Edit

Find 6 errors.

he grabed an old hotdog from a bin. wen we got back to the car he lookt a bit ill

Check
capital letters H + W   3 spell ✗
full stop .

Activity 8
Composition:
picture
prompts

What is the boy saying?

I'm so cross! Why has that dog ruined Grandad's slippers?

I'm so cross! Why has that dog gobbled up the beef and made a mess?

I'm so annoyed! Why is the dog on the bed?

Check capital letters   full stops   .   gaps

Activity 9
Composition

Power words
gobble
ruin
attack

a) **Make notes about Barker.**

👂 _____

👁 _____

♡ _____

🦵 _____

b) **Now write The bark in the dark.**

_____
_____
_____
_____
_____
_____
_____

Check
capital letters   full stops .   👆 gaps

Blue Storybook 2

See *Get Writing! Handbook* for lesson plans.

The poor goose

Activities 1, 2, 3, 4
Spelling

Green words

kn ow   r igh t   f or   h or se   sh ort

Red words

@ny   O th er   t wo   O ne   th ere

Your words

Activity 5
Hold a sentence

a

Check

capital letter   H   gaps
full stop   .   ed

6

b
_____
_____
_____

Check
capital letter H   gaps
full stop .   nn   ed   ng   ck

Activity 6
Build a sentence

miserable/miserably _____
_____
_____
_____
_____

Activity 7
Edit

Find 6 errors.

"that poor goose has no chance of wining she's short, and fet, and sillee!"

Check
capital letters T+S   3 spell ✗
full stop .

Activity 8

Composition: picture prompts

Think about some advice for a friend. Write some notes.

➡ What happened to them?

➡ How did they feel?

➡ Write your advice.

Check

capital letters   full stops **.**   gaps

8

Activity 9
Composition

Tell the story from the goose's point of view.

a)

b)

c)

Power words
scornful
insult
ignore
miserable
triumphant
thoughtful

Check
capital letters   full stops .   gaps

Blue Storybook 3

See *Get Writing! Handbook* for lesson plans.

Hairy fairy

Activities 1, 2, 3, 4
Spelling

Green words

hor se   kn ow   wr ap   ch air   most

Red words

c(ou)ld   th(ere)   (a)ll   th(ey)   (a)ny

Your words

Activity 5
Hold a sentence

 a

Check

capital letter   T   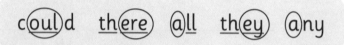 gaps
full stop   .   ch   ll

10

b
_____
_____
_____
_____

Check
capital letter   T   gaps
   full stop   .   th   ch

Activity 6 Build a sentence

despair _____
_____
_____
_____
_____

Activity 7 Edit

Find 6 errors.

the tooth fairy went upstairs he nippt into the bedroom and swappt a tooth for money

Check
capital letters T+H   2 spell   ✗
   full stops   ..

Activity 8
Composition: picture prompts

Write a newspaper report about what happened to the hairy fairy.

DAILY NEWS

Sacked again!
Fairy Queen in despair

No job joy!

Power words
disaster
despair
embarrassed

Check
capital letters   full stops .   gaps

Fairy Voice   July 18   Daily News 2

Hair despair

Fairy Queen quietly furious

13

Activity 9
Composition

ⓐ **Make notes about a perfect fairy and the hairy fairy.**

hair: _____

wings: _____

dress: _____

wand: _____

legs: _____

hair: _____

wings: _____

wand: _____

dress: _____

legs: _____

14

b **What does the Fairy Queen say a real fairy should be like?**

A real fairy

Blue Storybook 4

See *Get Writing! Handbook* for lesson plans.

Activities 1, 2, 3, 4
Spelling

Activity 5
Hold a sentence

King of the birds

Green words

fea th er   d ir t   th irsty   b ir d   wh irl

Red words

th(ei)r   s(o)me   t(o)   w(ou)ld   w(a)ter

Your words

a
_____

_____

_____

_____

Check

capital letter   H   gaps
full stop   .   tt   ed   th   pp

16

b
_____
_____
_____

Check
capital letter T   gaps
    full stop .   wh ed ff th ng

Activity 6
Build a sentence

quarrel _____
_____
_____
_____

Activity 7
Edit

Find 6 errors.

thirsty elephants, drinkin at the pond, squirtid their feathers with water. the crocs brusht the dirt off with their teeth

Check
capital letters T + T   3 spell ✗
    full stop .

17

Activity 8
Composition: picture prompts

a **Write about the birds.**

Hummingbird

Cockatoo

Parrot

Crow

Check
capital letters   full stops .   gaps

Power words
quarrel
argue
gorgeous
dull
ordinary

b) Who do you think should be King of the birds?

_____

_____

c) Who is the winner?

_____

Activity 9
Composition

Write about Crow and the other birds.

	Crow	Other birds
Behave and feel		
Sound like		
Move		
Look like		

19

Blue Storybook 5

See *Get Writing! Handbook* for lesson plans.

Our house

Activities 1, 2, 3, 4
Spelling

Green words

sch‿ool hou‿se c‿ou‿nt gr‿ou‿nd f‿ou‿nd

Red words

who all one watch does

Your words

Activity 5
Hold a sentence

ⓐ

Check

capital letter   M   gaps
full stop   .   ed   wh

20

b

_____

_____

_____

Check
capital letter   B   gaps
full stop   •   gg   ng

Activity 6
Build a sentence

cramped _____

_____

_____

_____

_____

Activity 7
Edit

Find 6 errors.

i'm in bed as i'm teling you all this it doesn't sound much, our house

Check
capital letters I+I+I   1 spell   ✗
full stops   ••

Activity 8
Composition: picture prompts

Write a letter to a friend you are going to stay with. Ask about his or her bedroom.

Dear _____ ,

Check
capital letters   full stops .   gaps

Activity 9
Composition

Power words
massive
heap
cramped
poky
overcrowded

Write about living in a small house, like the boy in the story.

My house is _____

_____

_____

_____

My house is so cramped that _____

_____

_____

Although my house is overcrowded _____

_____

_____

At times I wish my house was bigger, then __

_____

_____

When everyone is in the house _____

_____

23

Blue Storybook 6

See *Get Writing! Handbook* for lesson plans.

The jar of oil

Activity 1, 2, 3, 4 Spelling

Green words

bl<u>ow</u>   g<u>ir</u>l   l<u>i</u>v<u>e</u>   h<u>ou</u>s<u>e</u>   b<u>oy</u>

Red words

th<u>r</u>(ough)   (o)nc<u>e</u>   h(ere)   th(ere)   (wh)o

Your words

Activity 5 Hold a sentence

ⓐ

_____

_____

_____

_____

Check

capital letter   M   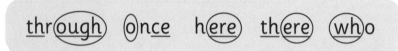 gaps
full stop   .   ss   ll   ng   ve

24

b
_____
_____
_____
_____

Check
capital letter   S   👆 gaps
   full stop   .   sh   ll   ve   ck

Activity 6
Build a sentence

elated _____
_____
_____
_____

Activity 7
Edit

Find 6 errors.

we will have a strong, handsome son his hair will be as blak as midnit, and his lips as red as a sunset

Check
capital letters W + H   2 spell ✗
   full stops   ..

25

Activity 8
Composition: picture prompts

Write an advert for the perfume. Give it a name. Write what it smells like and how it makes you feel.

Check
capital letters   full stops •   gaps

Activity 9
Composition

Write *thinking* and *happening* bubbles about the story.

Power words
elated
devastated
terrible
foolish
despair

Blue
Storybook 7

See *Get Writing! Handbook* for lesson plans.

Jade's party

Activity 1, 2, 3, 4
Spelling

Green words

same   face   take   place   made

Red words

brother   where   said   all   one

Your words

Activity 5
Hold a sentence

a

Check

capital letter   W   gaps
full stop   .   ed   ng

28

b

Check
capital letter W   gaps
full stop .

Activity 6
Build a sentence

delicious

Activity 7
Edit

Find 6 errors.

we must have picked up the rong shoping by mistake plastic bags all look the same to me

Check
capital letters W + P   2 spell ✗
full stops . .

29

Activity 8
Composition: picture prompts

Write about what type of class party you will have.

Party Planner

Theme:

Food:

Games:

Decoration:

Activity 9
Composition

Write an invitation for your class party.

Party Invitation

Dear _____

Please come to _____

_____

_____

_____

_____

_____

_____

From _____

Power words
delicious
exciting

Check
capital letters   full stops .   gaps

Blue Storybook 8

See *Get Writing! Handbook* for lesson plans.

Activity 1, 2, 3, 4
Spelling

Jellybean

Green words

Red words

Your words

Activity 5
Hold a sentence

a

Check
capital letter   W   gaps
full stop   .   sh   tch

32

b

Check
capital letter W
gaps
full stop .

Activity 6
Build a sentence

perfect

Activity 7
Edit

Find 6 errors.

its caj was easy to keep clean
it likt eating bits of cheese

Check
capital letters I+I   2 spell ✗
full stops . .

33

Activity 8
Composition: picture prompts

Decide which would be good pets and write a reply to the letter.

Dear Aunty Aggie,

I really want a pet but we have had a huge problem trying to get the right one. We had an elephant but it was too big and expensive to feed. The sheep bleated all night long. Then there was the mouse which escaped and gave Mum a terrible fright! Mum is at her wits' end and says I can have one more try. Which pet would you recommend and why?

3 best pets

1 _____

2 _____

3 _____

Best pet

_____

_____

Check capital letters   full stops .   gaps

34

Dear

Check

capital letters   full stops •   gaps

Activity 9
Composition

Power words
perfect
slimy
amazing

Write a poem asking for the perfect pet.

<u>Please, please, let me have a pet,</u>

Blue
Storybook 9

See *Get Writing! Handbook* for lesson plans.

A box full of light

Activity 1, 2, 3, 4
Spelling

Green words

white   nice   time   like   smile

Red words

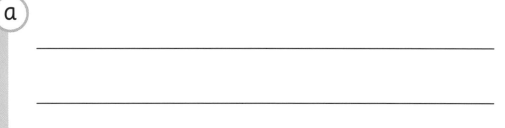

who   where   there   their   could

Your words

Activity 5
Hold a sentence

a
_____
_____
_____
_____

Check

capital letter   I   gaps
   full stop   .   speech marks   " "
exclamation mark   !

37

(b) _____

Check
capital letters L + F   gaps
full stop .   speech marks " "
apostrophe '   comma ,

Activity 6
Build a sentence

murky _____

_____

_____

Activity 7
Edit

Find 6 errors.

on the way bak, Kestrel had to rest fer a while Fox sat beside the box as she sleept

Check
capital letter O   3 spell ✗
full stops . .

38

Activity 8
Composition: picture prompts

Write a poem.

In the darkness

_____
_____
_____
_____
_____
_____
_____
_____
_____

Check

capital letters   full stops .   gaps

Activity 9
Composition

Power words
like lightning
as quick as a bullet
gloom/gloomy
pitch black
dim
murky

Beginning

Middle

End

Write the end of the story from Fox's point of view.

I released the sun

Blue Storybook 10

See *Get Writing! Handbook* for lesson plans.

The hole in the hill

Activity 1, 2, 3, 4
Spelling

Green words

spoke   chose   home   wrote   broke

Red words

your   any   could   what   their

Your words

Activity 5
Hold a sentence

a
_____
_____
_____
_____

Check

capital letter Y+I   gaps
full stop   .   ll

41

b _____

Check
capital letter   I   gaps
full stop   .   ll   ch

entice _____

Activity 6
Build a sentence

Activity 7
Edit

Find 6 errors.

The chilren came out of their homes they folloowed him up the hill the hole closed up.

Check
capital letter   T+T   2 spell   ✗
full stops   ..

Activity 8
Composition: picture prompts

Write a song to get the rats to follow you.

'Scamper up! Clamber up!
Rats, oh rats!
Gobble up and leave your homes,
Rats of Hamelin come with me,
To a place where you'll be free...'

_____

_____

_____

_____

'Scamper up! Clamber up!
Rats, oh rats!
Gobble up and leave your homes,
Rats of Hamelin come with me,
To a place where you'll be free...'

_____

_____

_____

_____

43

Activity 9
Composition

Write a letter, begging the Pied Piper to give the children back.

Power words
beg
demand
pity
entice

Dear Pied Piper,

44

Blue Non-fiction Book 3

See *Get Writing! Handbook* for lesson plans.

On your bike

Activity 1, 2, 3, 4
Spelling

Green words

while   time   ice   slide   safe

Red words

your   small   how   they   do

Your words

Activity 5
Hold a sentence

a

Check

capital letter   P   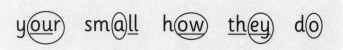 gaps

full stop   .   wh

45

b) _____

Check
capital letter C   gaps
full stop .   ck

Activity 6 Build a sentence

proud _____

Activity 7 Edit

Find 6 errors.

switch on your lights when you ride at nit be safe on your bik

Check
capital letters S+B   2 spell ✗
full stops ..

Activity 8
Composition: picture prompts

Connectives
first
next
then
after that

Write about learning to ride a bike.

When I learned to ride

Check

capital letters   full stops .   gaps

Activity 9
Composition

Write about how to take care of your bike.

handlebars:
_____
_____
_____
_____

wheel:
_____
_____
_____
_____

light:
_____
_____
_____
_____

chain:
_____
_____
_____
_____

Blue Non-fiction Book 5

See *Get Writing! Handbook* for lesson plans.

At the seaside

Activity 1, 2, 3, 4
Spelling

Green words

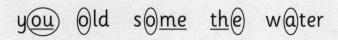

kite   beach   stone   sea   place

Red words

you   old   some   the   water

Your words

Activity 5
Hold a sentence

ⓐ

_____

_____

_____

_____

Check

capital letter   Y   gaps
full stop   .   th   ch

49

b

_____

_____

_____

Check
capital letter T   gaps
    full stop   .   ck

Activity 6
Build a sentence

predator _____

_____

_____

_____

Activity 7
Edit

Find 6 errors.

you can explore the caves on the bech you can sweem in the sea

Check
capital letters Y+Y   2 spell ✗
    full stops ..

Activity 8
Composition: picture prompts

Write a list of the ingredients you need for a picnic.

Check

capital letters   full stops .   gaps

Activity 9
Composition

Describe the things you can find in a rock pool.

Complex Speed Sounds

Consonant sounds

f	l	m	n	r	s	v	z	sh	th	ng
ff	ll	mm	nn	rr	ss	ve	zz	ti		nk
ph	le	mb	kn	wr	se		s	ci		
					c		se			
					ce					

b	c	d	g	h	j	p	qu	t	w	x	y	ch
bb	k	dd	gg		g	pp		tt	wh			tch
	ck				ge							
	ch				dge							

Vowel sounds

a	e	i	o	u	ay	ee	igh	ow
	ea				a-e	y	i-e	o-e
					ai	ea	ie	oa
						e	i	o
							y	

oo	oo	ar	or	air	ir	ou	oy	ire	ear	ure
u-e			oor	are	ur	ow	oi			
ue			ore		er					
ew			aw							
			au							

Red words to spell

I   the   said

me   he   be   we   she

no   go   so   put   was

were   want   of   you

your   my   to   are   her

all   small   some   they

one   there   their

Hold a sentence texts

Storybook 1: Barker
a) He started barking when we were all asleep.
b) He got the slipper and ripped it apart.

Storybook 2: The poor goose
a) He looked to the left and he looked to the right.
b) He grinned to himself as the cart bumped along the track.

Storybook 3: Hairy fairy
a) The hairy fairy sat on the chair all day.
b) There was hair on the floor and on the chair.

Storybook 4: King of the birds
a) He spotted some feathers that the birds had dropped.
b) The birds whirled off to their meeting.

Storybook 5: Our house
a) My head started to pound when he played his CDs.
b) Bounder was always digging up the ground.

Storybook 6: The jar of oil
a) My princess will have splendid rings on her fingers.
b) She will have gold around her neck.

Storybook 7: Jade's party
a) We raced along the pavement to the bus stop.
b) We made up party games on the way.

Storybook 8: Jellybean
a) We let the sheep sleep in the kitchen.
b) We had to feed the greedy beast.

Storybook 9: A box full of light
a) "I think it might be the light!" she said.
b) "Let's hide until the men go to sleep," said Fox.

Storybook 10: The hole in the hill
a) You stole from me and so I will steal from you.
b) I will steal your children.

Non-fiction Book 3: On your bike
a) Put on a helmet when you ride your bike.
b) Check the brakes on your bike.

Non-fiction Book 5: At the seaside
a) You can play with a kite on the beach.
b) Take a bucket and a spade to the seaside.

Get Writing! Blue Book 6

The **Get Writing! Books** contain a wide range of writing activities which are linked to the Storybooks and Non-fiction Books to make the strong link between reading and writing. Lesson plans for the writing activities are provided in the **Get Writing! Handbook**.

The writing activities and features include:

- Remembering and writing a sentence
- Finding spelling and punctuation errors in a sentence
- Composition activities which develop children's writing step-by-step from simple sentences to extended texts. Children write a variety of texts including: dialogue, recounts, non-chronological reports, instructions, descriptive texts, writing from experience, labels, poems and letters
- 'Check' boxes which prompt children to review their writing throughout
- Focus on 'power words' which encourages children to use ambitious vocabulary in their writing.

Use the **Get Writing! Books** with the Storybooks as follows:

Get Writing! Red Ditty Books 1–10	Red Ditty Books 1–10
Get Writing! Green Book 1	Set 1 Green Storybooks 1–10
Get Writing! Purple Book 2	Set 2 Purple Storybooks 1–10
Get Writing! Pink Book 3	Set 3 Pink Storybooks 1–10
Get Writing! Orange Book 4	Set 4 Orange Storybooks 1–12
Get Writing! Yellow Book 5	Set 5 Yellow Storybooks 1–10
Get Writing! Blue Book 6	Set 6 Blue Storybooks 1–10
Get Writing! Grey Book 7	Set 7 Grey Storybooks 1–13

Not to be photocopied

OXFORD UNIVERSITY PRESS

How to get in touch:
web   www.oxfordprimary.co.uk
email schools.enquiries.uk@oup.com
tel.   +44 (0) 1536 452610
fax   +44 (0) 1865 313472

ISBN 978-0-19-847907-9